Inspirational Bible Reflections

Inspirational Bible Reflections

Olga Quintero Franco

XULON PRESS

Xulon Press
2301 Lucien Way #415
Maitland, FL 32751
407.339.4217
www.xulonpress.com

© 2022 by Olga Quintero Franco

All rights reserved solely by the author. The author guarantees all contents are original and do not infringe upon the legal rights of any other person or work. No part of this book may be reproduced in any form without the permission of the author.

Due to the changing nature of the Internet, if there are any web addresses, links, or URLs included in this manuscript, these may have been altered and may no longer be accessible. The views and opinions shared in this book belong solely to the author and do not necessarily reflect those of the publisher. The publisher therefore disclaims responsibility for the views or opinions expressed within the work.

Unless otherwise indicated, Scripture quotations taken from the Holy Bible, New International Version (NIV). Copyright © 1973, 1978, 1984, 2011 by Biblica, Inc.™. Used by permission. All rights reserved.

Paperback ISBN-13: 978-1-66286-689-0

Table of Contents

The Miracle of Life 1

The Promise.................................. 15

The Reflection of the Holy Spirit 21

The Eternal Love............................... 25

The Spiritual Food 31

Life in Our Words 35

The Blessing of the World 39

The Renewal of the Sower 43

The Rock of Salvation............................51

Internal Health 55

Life in Jesus 61

Acknowledgements 67

The Miracle of Life

Ever since I had my first child, I have been able to see the miracle of life from God. When I was about to give birth my husband, my family, church members, and my pastor all accompanied me to the hospital. We all eagerly awaited the great, miraculous moment. I spent a whole day and part of the night in the hospital and still did not give birth. We prayed to God that everything would turn out well and that the child I was carrying in my womb would come out healthy.

At 2:21 am while I was in my pushing moments, a bright light appeared! I saw that it looked like an angel! Then I heard a voice say to me, "His name will be Ezekiel." My son then came out of my womb. I was surprised, because we hadn't chosen his name yet.

In those moments everything got complicated; well, time was running out and he wasn't breathing. He was going over his time…. doctors were doing everything to save my child and I was asking God to save him. Time passed and God saved him; He gave him life and breath. God wanted to glorify himself through that because my son was a miracle. About two days had passed and my pastor asked me what I had named my son. He said that while he was praying God had given him the name "Ezekiel". I explained my experience, that God had also given me that name. He confirmed the name for me! I know it was the Holy Spirit that had indicated and confirmed him. He was born in the year 1996.

A year and a half passed and I realized that I was carrying another baby. My husband and I wanted to have another child, a little brother for my first born. We wanted my children to grow up together, and so my second child was born five days after my husband's birthday. We named him after his paternal grandfather, Santiago. He was born very healthy and my home was full of joy. The day we dedicated the two of them at church, we also presented them to God together.

> "Children are an inheritance from the Lord, the fruits of the womb are a reward" (Psalm 127:3).

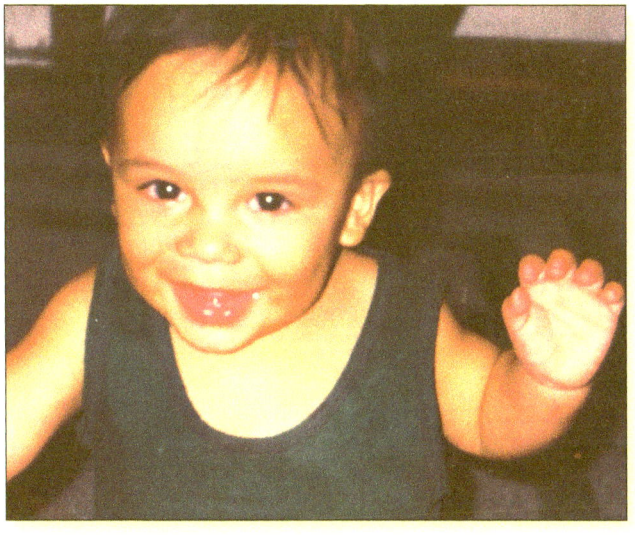

Having children of my own was a great joy. I have always had a very big heart for children. Three years had passed since Santiago's birth and to our surprise I was pregnant again. My husband and I prayed to God for a girl. When we went to the ultrasound, she hid and we had to go to another ultrasound later. At the second ultrasound, we were surprised to learn that we were going to have a princess! What joy! We started picking everything pink. God is good. Some tragic incidents happened during my pregnancy, but thank God I was able to have my princess at the right time. I gave birth to her on Thanksgiving Day. My heart filled with joy because of another little treasure. My two little boys and my princess!

Ten years passed and we were happy with our family. My sons were involved in sports and activities at school and my daughter took dance classes. But something was missing… I was a little sick and I was taking strong pills.

I didn't feel good taking them and wanted to stop, but the day I didn't take them, I felt even worse. If I didn't take them I felt very bad and couldn't sleep. I talked to my doctor one day and told him that my husband and I wanted to have another baby. He seriously told me that he did not recommend it to me. He said it was too risky and he couldn't take me off of the drug. My baby would be in danger.

A short time passed and in my heart I wanted another baby. I began to ask God for a miracle; rather, I implored him. I also wanted to feel better, because it felt like I was living a dream.

One day while I was praying, God gave me the courage and confidence to understand that He was going to accomplish my miracle. God was with me and was going to help me since I had faith. I depended on Him and not on my own strength. I had faith in Him and, although it had been impossible before, I knew that through Him the situation would be possible.

The day came—the test day to stop taking the pills and instead put my trust in Him. I didn't take them, and that same day I felt sick and sick and couldn't sleep that night. But I wasn't going to give up.

The next day passed and again I did not take the medication. I still felt bad and I talked to God. It was a time of anguish and trial and I said to God, "Lord, I believe in You and I know that You will answer my request. Although I am suffering now, I know that You will not forsake me.

You know my desire to stop taking medication and have another baby and I trust in Your power. Well, You are the Creator of the universe and the Author of life. I will depend on You and not on man."

On the third day of testing, I cried and prayed in my bedroom and spent time with God—just Him and me. Those moments were special, when God was dealing with my life and I began to have compassion for drug addicted people. I thought, *Maybe that's how they suffer and why they can't stop their drugs, or even some medicine. Oh my God, I have compassion for them now. Have mercy on them.* I was shivering from the cold and went to bed because I felt weak.

I fell asleep, and when I woke up I felt brand new. I knew that the miracle of my liberation had already arrived. I felt better, already liberated, and better than ever! The miracle He had been waiting for had arrived. I thanked God, and He made me feel His presence. Time ago was another chapter of my life. It was already in the past, and He wanted to glorify Himself in my total surrender to Him.

A year passed and we were on vacation in Texas when I started to feel some unusual cravings and disgust. I went for a pregnancy test at the store, and my husband and children were eagerly awaiting the results. There in Texas I realized that I was already expecting a baby; I was already three months into my pregnancy. My heart was full of joy and the whole family was happy. Our hearts were full of thanks to God.

> "What is impossible with men is possible with God" (Luke 18:27).

God allowed me to have another healthy son, without taking medication that would have affected him. He was born in 2010. We thought I was going to have another girl, but God wanted to give us another boy and we were happy with him and our very blessed home.

> "This is the child I asked of God, and he gave me" (1 Samuel 1:27).

That same year, when my baby was two months old, I spent time with God, reading His Word and praying. I felt in my heart to attend a college. I had previously been a parent educator in a Parents as Teachers program and had been a teacher's assistant for many years from pre-kindergarten through high school. In all of those schools I was an assistant, and in the church I was a teacher of many classes. I worked with different ages and various classes; I had been involved in the church since I was ten years old when I received salvation.

I wanted to study for something. I was spending very beautiful times with God in His presence, and one day I was on my knees in my living room, longing to listen to Him. He revealed himself to me and said, "My daughter, I know that you are hungry and thirsty for the Word of God and I know you want something new. My wish is that you continue to take time with Me and continue to read My Word. I will reveal to you My purpose in your life." In those moments I felt such a beautiful presence and I was super happy to continue spending time with God. I liked to study and read and learn more about the Bible since I was so inspired by the Word of God. I knew He had something special for me.

A few years passed and I began to write stories about God; stories from the Bible. I printed them and made folders, in both Spanish and English, and gave them to family members. I was inspired by the Word of God and I knew that God revealed His Word to me. I spent a lot of time with Him reading, praying and fasting. I had faith that the Word of God would touch the heart of the person who read that book.

My oldest children and my princess were still young, and my youngest was already four years old when I began to have symptoms of pregnancy. My children told me to take the test, although it was not planned and we were not expecting another baby. To my surprise I had already had a baby in my womb for five months! My husband and children thought, another girl? A little sister for my princess? The ultrasound showed that it was another son. Another miracle from God! With another child there would be four boys and a princess in the home. What happiness! Now our little boy would have a little brother to play with, since the other three were already older. He was born weighing six pounds, and what makes this even more special is that all my children were born weighing six pounds, all five of them. They only differentiated in the ounces. Every boy or girl that is born is a miracle of life; for God breathes the breath of life.

"Before I formed you in the womb, I had already chosen you" (Jeremiah 1:5).

Years passed and my youngest son, Matthew, was seven years old. He asked me why I was making binders. I told him that many years ago I used to make books and put them in binders but the computer had crashed and the copy of that particular book was lost. Although he wanted the book he had given away to be copied, everyone had already put it away because it had been such a long time.

I told him that a few weeks ago my aunt had visited me and I didn't expect what she gave to me. She told me, "Look what I have here!" It brought me great joy because my best wish was to publish my book. It was very special to me. I wanted to add to it according to what God revealed to me and to share His Word.

My son said to me with great joy, "Mom, keep going. Do not give up! One day I will see your book in a bookstore right?"

I told him, "God is great. Maybe yes, son. I will cherish your words and continue, Thank you for your words of encouragement." Actually, those words filled me with hope and motivation for another goal to move forward with God's purpose for my life. I was inspired by my youngest son to publish it and I hope that this book is not the last for the honor and glory of God.

My children and my daughter in 2019 at Santiago's wedding

"Children are an inheritance from the Lord, the fruits of the womb are a reward," (Psalms 127:3).

It has been an honor to have all my children. They are all special to me and each one has a special place in my heart. My grandchildren, not to mention… I love them! They are my everything….As the bible says, " Grandchildren are the Crown of the aged, and the glory of a son is his father. Proverbs 17:6

All of my children have challenged me to be a better person and a better mother. They were born with a purpose and I thank God for this great gift of being a mother. It is always nice to remember that everyone has different qualities, different personalities, different needs, and different goals and dreams. My greatest effort has always been to fill their minds and hearts with love and respect and also to fear God and love God with all their hearts. I always pray for them to have faith in God and never forget that they are a miracle of life, because every child that is born is a miracle. Actually, I tell them in this book that I love them and their father and I have tried to give them the best, and for us they are the most sacred and the most special thing in our lives. My prayers are that God's blessing always reaches them wherever they are, and that the God of miracles continues to be real in their lives. I have always thought that perhaps I will not leave them riches when God

calls me, but I will leave them the greatest treasure and wealth that is Jesus.

The relationship with Jesus is the greatest inheritance. With Him them they have everything! Thank you, God, for my children and grandchildren and for every miracle that is born. God is the God of miracles!

The Promise

From the beginning, God has always wanted us to have peace. When He made his image of Adam, He also wanted to make a companion, which is when He made the woman. God has always wanted well-being for us. He didn't want us to be alone. If we see it with human eyes, He wanted us to help each other.

When Jesus was here on earth, he promised us that the Holy Spirit would come and that the Comforter, who is God himself, would be with us until the end of the world. He promised that when His mission in the world was fulfilled, He was going to return, but He was going to prepare a place for us. It was a promise.

Many promises in Scripture were fulfilled. When Noah built the ark, a promise was fulfilled. God sent the flood because there was a lot of corruption, but He also promised never to send a flood again. That's why we have rainbows when it rains. The rainbow is a sign of promise that reminds us that we will never have a worldwide flood.

To the people of Israel, God promised to bring them out of Egypt and lead them to a promised land. Although it was forty years until they arrived, He never left them without food or drink and, although they became rebellious, God fulfilled His promise and they were able to reach the promised land.

God kept his promise to Abraham and Sarah and gave them a son in their old age. After Jesus came up from being on earth, He promised healing and now we can see that by laying our hands on the sick with faith there is healing. God has always kept His promises from the beginning of creation until the end! His Word shows us, even in our own lives, that His promises were fulfilled then and will be fulfilled now.

> If you love me, you will obey my commandments. I will ask the Father, and he will give you another Comforter to accompany you always: the Spirit of truth, whom the world cannot accept because it neither sees nor knows him. But if you know him, he lives with you and is in you. I am not going to leave you orphans: I will come back to you. Soon the world will not see me anymore, but you will see me. And because I live you will also live. On that day you will realize that I am in my Father, and you in me, and I in you. (John 14:15-20)

In the book of Matthew chapter 24, it says that in the last times there will be wars and rumors of wars, there will be famines and earthquakes everywhere. Nation will rise against nation, and everything will be the beginning of sorrows. Jesus also told His disciples to be careful and not to be deceived because they would come in His Name and say, "I am the Christ!" in order to deceive many.

> "Learn this lesson from the fig tree: As soon as its branches become tender and its leaves sprout, you know that summer is near. Likewise, when you see all these things, know that the time is near, at the doors. I assure you that this generation will not pass away until all these things take place. Heaven and earth will pass away, but my words will never pass away" (Matthew 24:32).

> "But as for the day and the hour, no one knows, not even the angels in heaven, nor the Son, but only the Father," (Matthew 24:36).

> "I'll make you a place. And if I go I'll prepare it for them, I'll come to take them with me. So you will be where I am" (John 14:3).

> "Therefore keep awake, for you do not know on what day the Lord will come," (Matthew 24:42).

The coming of the Son of Man is drawing near. This scripture will not fail us, neither will the Scripture and the signs—everything is written and everything will come to pass. As He says in His Word, we must prepare our hearts. Let's be ready, because it says in His Word that He will come like a thief in the night and will catch away those who are ready!

When the holidays come, many of us have the habit of decorating our houses, preparing our bank accounts to shop for the holidays, and even preparing what we are going to feast on for dinner. Now more than ever is the time to ready our hearts and wait for God. Every day, every minute we must meditate on his Word and be connected to His presence. Cell phones have to be charged to use them and wi-fi is needed to use the Internet; the same is true of the Holy Spirit. By accepting Christ, He lives in you. Every moment of communication with Him activates the Holy Spirit in you. In order to have a close relationship with another person, it is important to remain in regular communication with them. God is the person you should be in communication with the most. He is the Author of your life. Your destiny, your future, and your life depend on Him! No matter how far you have drifted from God, He has open arms, waiting to enter your heart and be the

Guide and Savior of your life. If you are on a bad path or even on the wrong path, it is time to make a decision and let God be the one to lead you towards the path of eternity.

There are two paths to choose from: Hell, where there is unbelief and rejection of God, where there will be no forgiveness and there will be consuming fire and suffering for eternity; or heaven, where there will be love, joy, peace and praise to God, and forever joy, pure happiness and there will be no more crying or pain. In the book of Revelation, he describes heaven where there will be streets of gold, crystal clear water, and best of all, we will be reunited with our loved ones forever. You can choose which path you follow now. The Bible says that it is better not to have known the truth or to have heard the truth, because already knowing you cannot have an excuse or you cannot say that you never listened. Every time someone surrenders to Christ, it is said in the Bible that there is a celebration in heaven, also for those who repent. Decide now. I will have a prayer of faith later in this book. Accept him today!

The Reflection of the Holy Spirit

Our faces always reflect how we feel. Sometimes we can tell how a person is feeling just by looking at them, without them saying anything, whether they are feeling sad or happy. When Moses spent time with God, his face reflected the glory of God. We know that with God we have peace. Sometimes, due to the circumstances of life, we only reflect sadness.

> "A merry heart is a great medicine, but a low spirit dries up the bones" (Proverbs 17:22).

The Word of God teaches us that David was sincere and even through his anguish worshiped God. David had the heart of God. The key to having peace and following it is to worship God as David did in any circumstance, even if it is very difficult. Remembering to worship God helps us to always have peace.

Psalm 34:1 tells us, "I will bless the Lord at all times, his praise shall be continually in my mouth. In the Lord shall my soul glory."

This verse reveals to us that if we don't focus on the problem and instead focus on God, our souls can boast. God's desire is that one always praises Him. He always has mercy on us.

Our face is like a mirror that reflects what we feel. If we spend time with God; if we always have communication with God in our minds and hearts, worshiping Him, we can rest and feel the fullness of peace in Him and reflect the Holy Spirit. God knows deep down what we truly feel, and He wants to give glory through whatever the need is. He will not leave you alone. He will send the comforter, the Holy Spirit, to bring you comfort and peace. His love and mercy are so great; just talk to Him .

We also know that the heart abounds and the mouth speaks. In this, we can understand how important it is to have peace. Above all things, when we worship God, He manifests Himself in our lives and we can always reflect a face full of the Holy Spirit.

> "So all of us, who with unveiled faces reflect the glory of the Lord like a mirror, are transformed into his likeness with more and more glory by the action of the Lord, who is the spirit," (2 Corinthians 3:18).

> "The Lord bless you and keep you: the Lord look upon you with favor and extend his love to you: the Lord show you favor and give you peace," (Numbers 6:24).

Every day unexpected things or situations arise. Sometimes we are having a good day when suddenly there is something or someone that ruins the moment. Not allowing that to ruin our day is learning, and at any moment you can decide to do good. Many times they say that it is better to stay quiet and give the problem to God, to say, "It is in your hands, God." You will be surprised what good God will work for in your life. Many times with the simple act of smiling at someone you can change the moment; just by saying something positive

you can even change someone's life. Smile now and decide to please someone and yourself. God is with you!

The Eternal Love

When Jesus died on the cross, He defeated the enemy. The law and condemnation under which we lived was removed. We know that He suffered and to the end defeated the enemy. His justice was fulfilled and the condemnation was also fulfilled then.

Eternal love was fulfilled in the crucifixion of Jesus. The scripture that was long awaited and said by the prophets was fulfilled when Jesus was raised up by his Heavenly Father. God showed His Spirit and still lives in us. Jesus came to show us in the flesh and in His own life how to live. He was always compassionate, kind, loving and merciful.

We can see and know that the love of a mother towards her child cannot be compared to any love. From the very beginning the serpent deceived the woman and it is the price that every woman now pays. He says in His Word that the woman will suffer labor pains; we can see that the woman suffers from many other things, but the greatest reason is for the love of a son or daughter.

The great love was Jesus. Jesus, in His own flesh, had mercy on the woman and the children. He removed the law that bound the human being, like the adulterous woman. Jesus removed all law in his death. He paid all condemnation so that we would have access to His kingdom. Everything is believing and having faith that God's plan is fulfilled in your life.

We are descendants of Abraham, because he is our father of faith. Abraham was our father of covenants who obeyed, giving his son in obedience, the son of promise in his old age. God wanted to know if Abraham would obey Him by asking Abraham to sacrifice his own son. He wanted to know if he really loved God and it was also prophetic that God was going to be glorified and the great covenant of faith was going to be shown through Isaac.

> After a certain time, God put Abraham to the test and said to him: "Abraham!" -"I'm here!" answered. And God ordered it: "Take your son, the only one you have and the one you love so much and go to the region of Moria. Once there, offer it as a burnt offering on the mountain that I will indicate to you."...
>
> Abraham took the wood of the burnt offering and put it on Isaac, his son, who, for his part, carried the fire and the knife. And the two kept walking together. Isaac said to Abraham: "Father!" Tell me my son,

"Here we have the fire and the wood,–continued Isaac, "but where is the lamb for the burnt offering?" The lamb, my son, will be provided by God."–Abraham replied And they continued walking together. When they arrived at the place appointed by God, Abraham built an altar and prepared the wood. Then he tied his son to Isaac and placed him on the altar, on top of the wood. So he took the knife to sacrifice his son, but at that moment the angel of the Lord shouted to him from heaven: "Abraham, Abraham!" "I'm here!" he answered. "Do not lay your hand on the boy or harm him," the angel told him. "Now I know that you fear God, because you have not even refused to give me your only son. Abraham looked up and, in a thicket, he saw a ram caught by the horns. It was then, he took the ram and offered it for the burnt offering instead of his son.

Genesis 22:1-2, 6-13

Abraham was our father of faith who also showed us his great obedience and his great sacrifice for God. It was afterward that God demonstrated His great love for us. In that act of obedience, he prophesied to us through

Abraham and Isaac. God recreated the life of Jesus on the cross. Isaac was a long-awaited promised son, and so was Jesus. Genesis 22:6 tells us that the wood of the burnt offering was taken and placed on Isaac. Jesus also carried his own cross. They were instruments of death that they carried on their backs. We can see in these two acts how the father obediently hands over his son in obedience. God showed us with this act of obedience what was going to happen next in the crucifixion of Jesus. God also provides the sacrificial lamb.

This story of Abraham and Isaac is a parable of the great redemption that God would one day accomplish with the life of Jesus. However, Isaac was not sacrificed because God was only testing Abraham and wanted to show His great love for His son, and show the great love of God that is Jesus. Jesus is the living sacrifice and we have redemption through Him and access to eternity in heaven.

God forgives humanity, demonstrating the great love that He has for us, by giving His only and beloved Son everything so that the Scripture and the great prophecy would be fulfilled. The ram was the exchange for Isaac's life, just as we were redeemed and Jesus already paid the price for us to live eternally together with Him .

Jesus marked us with his pact because he lived by faith, and with his sacrifices he showed his love for God. The son that Abraham was going to sacrifice was the great treasure. Jesus is the greatest treasure of the world. The great covenant was an assurance that we belong to God and are purchased with His blood.

<u>In his Word, he tells us to live and forgive with God's great love. He already covered every sin. If we are already marked with his pact, the great love of God, we do not have to wait or accept the mark of the end times that will be to surrender to the enemy. The great love was the death of Jesus and it is eternal. From the Old Testament we can see with this reflection that God showed us his love and his sacrifice for us through the life of his only Son, Jesus Christ. In Him we have redemption, healing, salvation, forgiveness of sins and access to eternity. His blood and his great love covers us. What great love the Father has given us that we are called his children!</u>

> "For God so loved the world that he gave his only begotten Son, so that everyone who believes in him may not perish, but may have eternal life" (John 3:16).

The Spiritual Food

We know that we need food to eat and drink. God made us like this. If we don't have these two things in our lives for a long time we will start to feel weak.

God also created us to hunger and thirst for spiritual food. His Word says that Jesus is the spiritual food that leads us to eternal life. Before dying on the cross, Jesus and his disciples ate the sacrament. It was a demonstration of what we should do in our lives, and to do it continually as a reminder.

Jesus is the bread of life and his blood is what cleanses us from all sin. The bread is his body and the juice represents the blood he shed for us. This demonstration is the new covenant between God and the person. It is being aware that you are waiting for him to come and have a life with Him.

> "Certainly I assure you–affirmed Jesus–that if you do not eat the flesh of the Son of man or drink his blood, you do not really have life. He who eats my flesh and drinks

my blood has eternal life, and I will raise him up on the last day" (John 6:53-54).

"I am the living bread that came down from heaven. If anyone eats of this bread, he will live forever. This bread is my flesh, which I will give so that the world may live" (John 6:51).

In Jesus, we have life and life in abundance; it is a promise that one day it will return. His blood cleanses us and gives us power, because He gives power and freedom. His blood removes all condemnation and He has already paid the price for all sin. He was just and dignified in giving his blood for us, and by paying with his human body, our sicknesses and diseases were healed. It is the liberation of the children of God. The vinegar that Jesus took was a symbol that we will never thirst, because we have the Holy Spirit who is with us, and His Word feeds us.

Jesus also told his disciples at the Lord's Supper, "This is my blood of the covenant, which is shed for many for the forgiveness of sins. I tell you that I will not drink of this fruit of the vine from now on, until the day that I drink with you the new wine in my Father's kingdom" (Matthew 26:28-29).

"Certainly he bears our diseases and bears our pains, but we consider him wounded, beaten by God and humiliated. He was pierced for our transgressions, and crushed for our iniquities; on him fell, the punishment, the price of our peace, and thanks to his wounds we are healed," (Isaiah 53:4-5).

We must remember that if we confess our sins, He is faithful and just and forgives us. But let us also not forget that we have to forgive all those who have offended us. He says in His Word that for Him to forgive us, we also have to forgive everyone, even if it is the hardest thing we do. It is an act of obedience.

Now and always we will remember his crucifixion; now and always we are free from everything the enemy

wants to bring to us. We are free because He has already paid for our illnesses. He already paid for our sins. He redeemed us with His blood. The word of God that feeds our being, our soul, our spirit will fill us and strengthen us. Many times we feel that something is missing and we even feel weak, without strength, without the will to live. We need to feed our lives with God's food; with Jesus, the spiritual food. He will bring strength and purpose to your life. Let Him fill your being, your soul, your heart and your mind. Remember that Jesus was also resurrected and we must wait for him every day!

Life in Our Words

Every time we speak, we have power in our words. For example, when a baby says his first word we feel so much joy that he has already used his power of speech. Or, take the example of a Judge. When they tell us the verdict, we feel the anxiety from hearing the word of power.

Even when we are away from a family member or close friend and we hear their voice on the phone, it makes our hearts happy. We know that our words bring life or bring death; encourage or discourage; rise or drop. The simple act of telling someone that you love them brings consolation, but telling them that you hate them brings sadness.

Jesus had authority to pick up a cripple, saying, "Pick up your mat. Get up and go!" Jesus has the truth in his words. Everything he said was prophecy and what he said was going to happen has happened or is yet to happen. Once upon a time Jesus calmed a storm with his own words and authority.

> Then he got into the boat and his disciples followed him. Suddenly a storm broke out on the great lake so strong that

the waves flooded the boat. But Jesus was asleep. The disciples went to wake him up. -Lord–they shouted -, save us that we are going to drown! "Men of little faith," I reply, " why are you so afraid? Then Jesus got up and rebuked the winds and the waves, and everything was completely quiet. (Matthew 8:23-26)

As I reflect on this passage my question is, what storm have you experienced that Jesus has already calmed? Or what storm are you going through that Jesus only asks you to have faith and never be afraid? He is with you as he was with his disciples. He already knew there was a storm; I think that even He already felt the waves. He wanted his disciples to have faith in him . They had seen the miracles that Jesus made possible through the power of God. Let's look at God and His power—the calm will come and the storm will go. All it takes is for you to ask Him to be with you through that storm and give you faith. Put your trust in Him and He will work. Jesus wants to be with you on that boat. He is the Almighty! It is so important to reflect when we come out of the storm on what we have learned or what God wants to teach us, because in weakness God makes us stronger.

It says in the book of John that Jesus did the work so that they would believe in Him, so that they would know and understand that the Father was in Him and He was in the Father. Jesus also has life in his words. He himself said, "I am the resurrection and the life. Whoever believes in me will never die" (John 11:25). Jesus said that if we abide by him and his words abide in us, that we can ask whatever we wanted, and it would be granted (John 15:7).

Jesus is the true vine; we are the branches. If we let Jesus and His Word remain in us, then we will always have the blessings that Jesus had, because God Himself will dwell in us.

> "May my words and my thoughts be acceptable to you, O Lord, my rock and my redeemer!" (Psalm 19:14).

By meditating on the scripture and the blessings of being in communication and praying on God, we will be in His presence and that will help us so that no corrupt word comes out of our mouth. We will all give an account to God for every corrupt word that comes out of us. In Matthew 12:37 it says that by our words we will be acquitted and by our words we will be condemned.

> "He who is good produces good out of the goodness he treasures in his heart; but he who is wicked produces evil out of his wickedness, for out of the abundance of the heart the mouth speaks" (Luke 6:45).

<u>Let's be a blessing and not a curse. If God dwells in your life, your words will also bring life, power, authority, healing, and truth. Just believe in Him, without hesitation. The word of God is inspired by God and each word builds up our soul. Declare blessings and let their words bring life. Your words can bring healing to the heart if you let God work. God will bring life into your words!</u>

The Blessing of the World

Ever since Adam sinned, the earth has been cursed. Therefore, he did not obey God and instead trusted the woman. The woman trusted and believed the snake. They were deceived and each one suffers—the woman suffers giving birth and the man suffers iin his work (he will give the sweat of his brow) and the serpent will eat dust all the days of his life. Eve was deceived because she wanted to know more than God. In the ten commandments, it tells us in one that we honor and worship only God. We shall have no idols.

Each person can bless our land, as it is cursed. God expects us to believe in Him and His power. He wants us to honor Him in spirit and in truth. When we stop honoring other things and totally depend on Him and not on man, we do not give any power to anyone else. He made the earth and He can't bless it if we don't give Him the honor. Therefore, He made us, and the earth and all its fullness is His . Let's stop depending on man. We look at our lives and leave everything that can be an idol for us. In the evil day, He will deliver us and rescue us from the evil one. When we obey the commandments and do not let the enemy deceive us with any false idols, we will be blessed.

The earth has left God, has forgotten God and has believed in other idols; therefore, the land has been cursed. God wants to bless us. God wants to manifest His power and His love, since we are in the last times. He is a God of mercy and wants His salvation to reach every door of the human heart. Miracles will manifest and the earth will be blessed when each one unites and fights so that the name of God may once again be honored in this world. We have to fight so that Christ dwells first in our lives, and then dwells in this world. The honor belongs to God. Jesus already paid the price. It is up to us to fight for Him. Man always wanted to know more than God, but God is the Creator and the Author of life. God created you. Bring Him honor!

> Do not have other Gods besides me. Do not make for yourself any idol, nor anyone who bears a resemblance to what is in heaven above, nor to what is on earth, nor to what is in the waters under the earth. Do not bow down to them or worship them. I the Lord your God, am a jealous God. When parents are evil and hate me, I punish their children to the third and fourth generation. On the contrary, when you love me and keep my commandments,

The Blessing of the World

I show you my love for a thousand generations. (Exodus 20:3-6)

If you obey the Lord your God, all blessings will come upon you and will accompany you always: "Blessed will you be in the city, and blessed in the field. Blessed will be the fruit of your womb, your crops, the young of your cattle, the calves of your herds and the lambs of your flock. Blessed will be the basket and your kneading table. Blessed shall you be at home and blessed on the way. The Lord will grant you victory over your enemies" (see Deuteronomy 28).

"But the time is coming, and has now come, when true worshipers will worship the Father in spirit and truth , for that is the way the Father wants those who worship him to be" (John 4:23).

"I'm the way, the truth and the life; no one comes to the Father except through me" (John 14:6).

If we listen to the will of the Father, we can know what God wants us to do for our earth. Each one can change and bring healing and blessing to our land. Let the name of Jesus dwell on this earth. He is your salvation and the salvation of the world. Do not choose the curse for you and those you love most. God wants to bless you!

The Renewal of the Sower

The Bible teaches us to always sow a good seed. We know that only a seed produces good fruit, especially when it is planted in good soil. The seed is the Word of God.

Scripture also teaches us of renewal. The question is, how can we have good fruit and sow on good soil? The answer: when we change course and follow Jesus. When we surrender our lives to Him and sincerely give Him the will of our lives, He automatically begins to work in our lives. The Holy Spirit is activated in our lives.

The way to let the Holy Spirit work in us is to believe; believe that He is working in us without hesitation. Something that puts a barrier so that the Holy Spirit does not work is doubt or lack of forgiveness. Maybe we are right and sometimes we are so hurt, or the seed is not planted in good soil. Jesus can refresh and renew. You can begin to bear good fruit and your roots will change. When you give everything to Him, He will change things. It can change your life when you give everything to Him and forgive with the forgiveness of Jesus. This is how you develop strong roots and begin to sow good seed. Under those circumstances, you bear much fruit because your heart is renewed with Jesus. Life is Jesus. People want what you have because they can see and feel it. The moment you plant, it is watered. Jesus is the Sower who renews your life and your heart.

> When someone hears the word about the kingdom and does not understand it, the evil one comes and snatches away what he sown in his heart. This is the seed sown along the way. The one who received the seed that fell on rocky ground is the one who hears the word and immediately receives it with joy; but since it has no root; it lasts a short time. When trouble or persecution arises because of the word, he immediately turns away from it. The one who received the seed that fell among thorns is the one who hears the word, but the worries of this life and the riches choke it, thus it does not come to bear fruit. But the one who received the seed that fell on good ground is the one who hears the word and understands it. This one does produce a harvest at thirty, sixty and even a hundredfold. (Matthew 13:18-23)

Once upon a time I was going through a very difficult test. I was praying for this situation, but my prayers were not getting answered. I was already desperate. One day I was already frustrated and told a family member, "I don't want to live anymore. Why live if I'm going through this?"

It was a very difficult situation that already made me desperate, but the moment I said those words aloud, that person rebuked me. I felt that at that moment I failed as a person and as a mother. I had lost all my faith in God. I didn't think anything of it until a few weeks had passed and my health was deteriorating. Something had happened to me that required seeing a doctor. While crying and meditating at night, God reminded me of that night that he had said he didn't want to live. It was then that I picked up the phone and recognized that I was wrong to express myself like that and apologized to the person who I had said that to. Maybe we go through despair sometimes. At that moment, what came out of my mouth was not a blessing, but a curse.

I spent months seeing doctors until God told me to depend totally on Him. Doctors, therapists, and chiropractors gave me a different diagnosis, but my life changed for the better through that experience. I began to totally depend on God's answer and not on man. I knew that experience was God in my life. It was frustrating to go to the doctor, since there was no solution, but God was working in my life. Months passed, up to half a year, and one day I said to God, "Now yes, I totally depend on You, but my situation has not changed."

I heard a voice say to me, "Have eyes of faith!"

At that moment, I thanked God and began to see my situation with eyes of faith. While my faith grew and I looked at everything with eyes of faith, although it was not easy all the time, everything began to change. God was healing my heart and then I was solving the problem. Sometimes we pray for a situation to change, but how is our heart? Are we fully trusting and depending on Him with eyes of faith? When I was unforgiving and doubtful of God, He could not work in my life.

One day while I was praying, I was having very beautiful times with God. I told him that I was going to tell this testimony and I was going to publish this experience in my book. As I spent time with God that day, I knew it was another page in my life, another chapter that had passed. God gave me the understanding that the will was to change me first. Here's a thought for you: *Working hard for something that doesn't matter is called stress. Working hard for something we love is called passion.* It is my passion to be able to share!

Jesus is not a story. It's real! It can live in your life and change your life so that you have good roots and bear fruit. He will work in your life. Believe in Him and give Him everything, especially what has hurt you. God is just and will fight for you.

Our deeds demonstrate the seed we planted. God wants you to be a blessing to others. He cares about your life! He will renew you and give you good roots and every seed He sows will bear fruit. Jesus is the renewal of your heart.

> The one who supplies the seed to the one who sows will also supply bread for you to eat, will increase the crops and will cause you to produce an abundant harvest of righteousness. You will be in every way so that on every occasion you can be generous, And so that through us your generation will result in thanksgiving to God. (2 Corinthians 9:10-11)

I am going to tell you something that I taught my princess when she was little. I told her, "Sometimes you feel like you have a lot of burdens and you feel like you don't know what to do about your problems. Don't feel alone; write them on the tablet of your mind or heart in prayer, or perhaps on a piece of paper and put them in a box." And she did what I told her. She wrote down her requests and made a little box and put them inside. I told her, "Now take your little box and put it up, you taking the little box up, and tell God, 'Here are my requests, Jesus. I believe in You that you will take them. You will help me because I believe in You and you say in your Word to cast my cares upon you. Thank you Jesus. I love you!'"

It is an act that I taught my daughter and she remembers. I say the same right now. You may not have to make a little box, but in your prayers give Him everything—all of your burdens. It is important to know that you are special to God. Then I told her, "After praying for your requests, put your little box in a place like a closet or under the bed and forget about it for a while. Then you go back and read your petitions and thank God for the ones that were answered and the ones that were not… have faith." My daughter tells me that she is grateful for this act that I taught her since it has helped her in her walk with God.

> "Finally, the fruit of justice is sown in peace for those who make peace," (James 3:18).

> "My brothers, consider yourselves very happy when you are faced with various tests.

> For you know that the testing of your faith produces perseverance" (James 1:23).

> "Trust in the Lord with all your heart, and not in your own intelligence. In all your ways acknowledge him, and he will make your paths straight" (Proverbs 3:5-6).

Perhaps you have lost faith or focus on God. God wants to restore your life and make every seed you plant is a blessing. There are times when we are tested and sometimes we feel like we can't take it anymore, but remember that you can depend on God. God's will is that we let God work in our lives. Maybe it will change the direction of your life. God wants you to depend totally on Him . We cannot change and control the situation by ourselves. Even if things are not perfect or easy, trust Him. Leave it all to God, and He will work in your life!

The Rock of Salvation

From the beginning, it was God of creation who created the world. And if we have respect for our parents, how much more can we have for God? He certainly tells us in His Word that to fear God is to have wisdom. To fear God is to have respect for Him; to have respect for Him is to recognize who He really is.

Scripture tells us how David was able to defeat a giant. The giant was trying to kill David, and David was much smaller than Goliath. David was looking for a way to flee, but the way to get rid of that giant was to stone him.

David grabbed a rock and with one throw at it, Goliath fell instantly. David hit him on the forehead and he died instantly. It was unbelievable, but God was on David's side and had his back because David feared God. David loved God and that giant was evil. The rock was David's salvation.

When Jesus was on earth, He talked to the people and taught them the Word of God. When the Jews heard, they stoned Jesus. It was a way of condemning.

The Scripture teaches us that there was an adulterous woman and the rulers of the people accused her and tried to stone her. They said, "Well, if the law of Moses tells us to do such a thing to an adulterous woman!" But Jesus said to them, "Are any of you without sin? Let him who is without sin cast the first stone!" There was no one without sin and no stone was cast. The stone was a way to condemn and break the law.

His Word is like the rock. We know that the rock is strong and does not move. So is Christ, because He is the Savior of the world. He came to save and did not come to condemn the world.

> "Because God loved the world so much, that he gave his only begotten son, so that everyone who believes in him may not perish, but may have Eternal Life. God did not send his Son into the world to condemn the world, but to save it through him" (John 3:16-17).

The rock was David's salvation. The rock saves us from great giants and mistakes in life that want to condemn us. The rock is Christ!

They wanted to condemn Jesus by throwing rocks at him, but Jesus came to save the world, dying on the cross. He freed us from all condemnation. He didn't let the adulterous woman be stoned because He was going to pay the ultimate price for all of mankind's sin.

"How much I love you, Lord my strength! The Lord is my rock, my shelter, my deliverer; It is my God, the rock in which I take refuge. It is my shield the power that saves me, my highest hiding place!" (Psalm 18:1-2).

"God is my salvation and my glory; it is the rock that strengthens me; my refuge is in God," (Psalm 61:7).

Let the Rock of salvation be Christ. He is the high and solid foundation, He is immovable and He is greater than the greatest source of strength! He will give His protection more than any mountain. Jesus is the Rock where salvation is found. He is the Savior of the world and He came to save.

Internal Health

Life is Beautiful. God has given us His Word, which is the Bible, and it helps us live a life that pleases Him. The Bible is our guide, our map, our direction to life that if we live in His will. We can live trusting that He will support us in everything.

But what do we say when some circumstances or decisions do not please God? Perhaps we are living a life serving God, but nothing seems to go right for us. Or perhaps you are in doubt or disbelief. He is so close to you and wants to be a part of your life.

Once, a boy asked his father if God was as big as the plane that was passing through the sky. Was God so close? Then the father took the boy to an airport and said, "Son, do you see the plane?"

The boy told him, "Yes!"

He said, "God is like this plane! God is great and powerful and he is as close as you have him."

Some feel God close while some feel God far away. The plane was the same plane that was flying in the air that first day the boy had seen, but now he was looking at the plane more closely. Like that reflection, that is how God wants to be in your life. He wants to be close.

In this book full of Scripture and reflections from God, I hope that you can feel God as close as I feel to Him while writing it. I hope that as you read it, you know God for who He really is—a loving God who cleanses, forgives, restores, heals, strengthens, comforts, and fills your life with blessings beyond abound.

Perhaps you have experienced the loss of a family member, or a child, or a friendship. Maybe you lost a father or a mother and feel that life has no meaning. Maybe you're sick with a disease that even doctors don't have the cure to. Maybe something or someone in your life has completely let you down. Perhaps someone has hurt you and you have roots of bitterness. There can be so many things that are afflicting you; even the lack of forgiveness. Sometimes we can't even forgive ourselves when God is at the door, waiting for us to open our hearts to carry every burden, every disease, and everything that hinders us to be the God of our life. More than anything, He wants to heal our being and our heart.

In the Bible, there was a paralytic who needed healing. The paralytic was on a stretcher and had never walked. There were so many people around that they put it up on the roof and made a hole in the house to lower it down for Jesus to see. When Jesus saw him he said, "Son, your sins are forgiven." They were all surprised to hear what Jesus had said and wondered by what authority he had said that. Jesus said, "What is easier, to say to the paralyzed man, 'Your sins are forgiven!' or tell him, 'Get up, grab your stretcher and walk'? Well, so that they know that the Son of Man has authority on earth to forgive sins, he then addressed the paralytic. "I say to you, get up, take your stretcher and go home." He got up, took his stretcher right away and walked out in full view of everyone. They were amazed and began praising God (see Mark 2:5-12).

This paralytic Bible passage brings a great revelation of inner healing. First, God wants to heal us and forgive our sins to free us from every bondage. What we carry in our hearts, we transfer to our minds. Sometimes we bring generational curses, but God can work and heal and free you from every curse and He can and wants to heal your heart first. Do not hesitate. Spend intimate time with Him in prayer and open your heart; He will work in your life. Just believe in Him with all your heart. Give him your heart. When you are ready, confess your sins to Him and He will cleanse you.

Perhaps He will show you something or someone that you have hurt, and you need to heal. You need to forgive with the love and forgiveness of Jesus. Give Him everything! Have faith in God that everything will work in your life for blessing. The plan is perfect and the day has come— surrender all to Him. Your burdens are no longer yours. God will already be your God when you ask Him to enter your heart and reign and be the God in your life.

As a newlywed, I went to a church event and walked down the aisle after a sermon that spoke to my life. I was at the altar having some intimate time with God, and there He showed me in the bottom of my heart that I had been hurt.

Years passed and one day I handed a letter of forgiveness to the person who had hurt me. I handed a letter to the person God taught me to forgive. In that letter I was showing my forgiveness and God's forgiveness. The healing was for Him and for me! I had to be free and I was obedient. God wants to heal your heart so that you can be free. Where there is healing, there is freedom!

Don't forget your relationship with Him. As a plant needs water to grow and live, we need the Word of God to grow and live. Our being needs and yearns for God. He is at the door of your heart.

> **Here I am! I stand at the door and knock. If anyone hears my voice and opens the door, I Will come in and eat with that person and they with me. Revelation 3:20**

INTERNAL HEALTH

The Lord is my Shepherd. I lack nothing. He makes me lie down in green pastures, he leads me beside still waters, he refreshes my soul. He guides me along the right paths for his names sake.
Psalm 23:1-3

Our Internal Health is the most important tool to take care of; it is where our life is. The bible says it's the wellspring of life and we must guard our heart. It brings us understanding and if we acknowledge God and keep His Will in our life and always ask him for understanding. He is there to guide us along the way and heal our heart. Letting God deal with your heart and communicationg with Him and letting Him abide in your heart is the best to a good life. Many times we

lean on our own understanding on not on Gods, but if we acknowledge Him and His understanding He will be there to lead the way. A blessed life! Let God enter your heart and let His Will be done in your life today… in all that you do acknowledge Him… you won't regret it!

Life in Jesus

When Jesus was born, we know that it was the Holy Spirit who brought him into the world. From that moment when Jesus was born on, what the Scripture said was fulfilled—that we have life in Him.

Before the birth of a baby, the time it lasts in the womb is the time when God works. The great miracle that God does in forming the baby is the miracle of life. At the moment the baby is in the mother's womb it already has life, but when it comes out into this world, everything is transformed for the baby. Everything takes time to form.

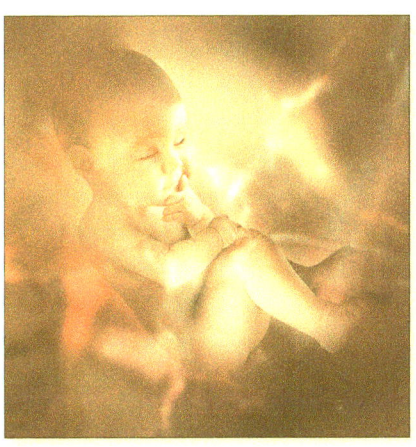

Something very important that we must know is that God is working in the womb, and in time everything will be formed so that the baby comes out on time. The Holy Spirit is the one who works in the mother and the baby. It is the Holy Trinity, since all three work in one: God the Father, Jesus the Son, and the Holy Spirit. Likewise, it is the same image of the mother when she is going to give birth: the mother, the baby, and the Holy Spirit.

> "You created my entrails; you formed me in my mother's womb. I praise you because I am an admirable creation! Your works are wonderful, and this I know very well! My bones were not unknown to you when I was formed in the innermost recesses, when I was woven together in the depths of the earth" (Psalm 139:13-15).

When we come to know Jesus as our Savior, our lives are transformed and we are reborn. As babies, we need our spiritual milk, which is the Word of God.

> "Long for the pure milk of God's word, like newborn babies. Thus through her you will now grow in your salvation" (1 Peter 2:2).

As we grow, our food intake increases and we need solid foods in order to grow. The Scripture is fulfilled, which says:

> "Truly I say to you, whoever hears my word and believes him who sent me has eternal life and will not be judged, but has passed from death to life" (John 5:24).

In John 3:3 Jesus tells Nicodemus, "Truly I say to you, anyone who is not born again cannot see the kingdom of God."

Being born again is a work of God and it is a miracle. The Holy Spirit comes and dwells in us, becoming the heritage of Jesus. Let the miracle of life be a part of you. Life in Jesus is when you begin to live and not only do you have the Holy Spirit that guides you, but you feel fullness of peace that comes to transform your life.

> "But to all who received him, to those who believed in his name, he gave the right to become children of God. These are not born of blood, nor by natural desires, nor by human will, but of God" (John 1:12-13).

Keeping God in mind and being a child of Him is a very great privilege. It is the best decision you can make. You will always have the Holy Spirit to accompany you in every step you take, and every decision you make will be because you are convinced of the truth. Now it is not only, "If it is your will, Lord;" now it is to take it into account and always make the right decision. We are an inheritance from Him. He has a purpose for each person and He wants the best for you.

> "If you confess with your mouth that Jesus is Lord, and believe in your heart that God raised him from the dead, you will be saved. For with the heart one believes to be justified, but with the mouth one confesses to be saved" (Romans 10:9-10).

> "My sheep hear my voice; I know them and they follow me. I give them eternal life, and they shall never perish, nor can anyone snatch them out of my hand" (John 10:27).

> "Blessed is the one who resists temptation, because when he is approved, he will receive the crown of life that God has promised to those who love him" (James 1:12).

Accept Him today. If you wish to accept Christ as your only and beloved Savior, repeat this prayer:

Lord Jesus, I thank you for loving me, for offering me an abundant and happy life. Today I recognize that I am a sinner, I have made mistakes and I repent. I beg you to forgive me, and to cleanse me from all evil. I believe in you Jesus. I believe that when you died on the cross, you did it to give me salvation, to give me a happy and eternal life with you. On this day I accept Your forgiveness. I ask you to give me the gift of life which is eternal life. Thank you for Your salvation, for being my King and giving me life in abundance. I believe in Your promise that one day I will live forever with You in heaven. Today I receive you. Thank you Jesus. Amen.

Acknowledgements

I would first like to thank God for this accomplishment of publishing my books. Without Him, this could not be posible! He is not only my Savior, my life, my inspiratation…he's my All! In any reality I never imagined this plan for my life but He makes all things possible! God is full of surprises!

I want to thank my parents and my sister. Your love not only helped me grow, but your protection always made me feel secure. I love you guys so much. I always pray God's blessing upon your lives. Daddy I miss you I know u left earth but you will forever stay in my heart… I love you daddy!

A big part of my life and one of the biggest blessings is my husband, the love of my life, and my children. They the biggest blessings in my life. I have so much to be grateful for them. I want to give a special thanks to my son Ezekiel for always being there for me in anything I need for my book and in promoting my book … I appreciate you mijo.

I want to thank a very special person… Rosa. My dear best friend and soul sister who was a very big part of my life growing up(since Kinder). She is not here as she passed away in 2018… I will never forget our friendship and the happiness she brought to me. It was a friendship that was so special. I wanted to acknowledge and tell you all about her because a year before she passed away she asked me while on a phone call, "What are your goals, your dreams, or what do you most think of?" I said, "I have it in my heart to share with everyone the love that God has for each person… I would love for people to know God as their personal savior before He returns."

As I said that, I had not yet dreamed about publishing a book; I had only made binders years before filled with stories. That conversation meant a lot as I go back and remember because that is the whole purpose of me publishing my book, is to share God's love and for you to find God's purpose for your life, but most of all for Him to bring Salvation. I ovcourse miss her tremendously. I will always remember and cherish her in my heart.

I hope this book has been a blessing to your life, but most of all brought you closer to God as He loves you and wants to be the God of not just today but your future and eternity. Be blessed! God bless you!

CPSIA information can be obtained
at www.ICGtesting.com
Printed in the USA
JSHW030339291222
35483JS00007B/56